I0163638

Deception
In Gospel
Presentation

Larry Adams

Copyright © 2019 Larry Adams, All Rights Reserved

Scripture quotations marked (NASB) are taken from the New American Standard Bible®, Copyright © 1960, 1962, 1963, 1968, 1971, 1972, 1973, 1975, 1977, 1995 by The Lockman Foundation Used by permission." (www.Lockman.org)

Dictionary Quotations marked (CG-ED) are from the Concise Greek-English Dictionary of the New Testament Prepared by Barclay M. Newman, Jr., (c) 1971 United Bible Societies,(c) 1993 Deutsche Bibelgesellschaft, Stuttgart. Used by permission.

Dictionary Quotations marked (CWSB Dictionary) are taken from the Complete Word Study Bible Dictionary Copyright © 2003 by AMG Publishers. All rights reserved.

Dictionary quotations marked (Greek-English Lexicon, The - by Louw & Nida) are taken from The Greek-English Lexicon, by Louw, Johannes P. and Nida, Eugene (1988) by The American Bible Society

Contents

Books by Larry Adams

How Does God Express His Sovereignty?
Six Biblical Issues Against "God Is In Control"
Discipling A New Believer
Revelation: A Fresh Perspective
Future Focus
Did You Ever Realize
That Your Prayers May Not Be Hindered
Out On A Limb

BASIC CONCEPTS

I've read many books and articles about how to study the Bible and interpret it and come to a good understanding of what is written. Two of those items were books on Hermeneutics, the so-called "science" of interpretation." These turned out to be very long and almost bored me to tears. Not to mention how convoluted and complex the "rules and regulations" turned out to be. I have also read books on translation and have several books regarding the wording and grammar of the original Hebrew and Greek in which the Bible was written. All these things help in their own way, but all seem to be collections made by people. I'm not throwing out hermeneutics, but eventually I found a few things within the Bible that clue us into how God wants us to handle the interpretation, understanding, and application of his word. These things are the most basic things possible but are never taught in the church – at least not that I have been able to discover. But, first we'll start with what amounts to basic reading fundamentals.

9 Rules of Interpretation

1. Rule of Definition

Define the terms to be used and keep to those terms and that definition. Terms should be defined as they were understood in the first century and before.

2. Rule of Usage

The Bible was written by Jewish prophets and the terms used were understood within the context of the ancient Jewish culture. The usage of terms in modern discussions should reflect how the terms were used then and not according to any modern culture.

3. Rule of Context

Context is the surrounding words, phrases, paragraphs, and concepts of a particular phrase, word, or sentence under examination. The context lends understanding to what is under discussion. The local context should take priority over any other context elsewhere in the Bible that might be of a similar subject except when the local context does not provide any understanding for the item under discussion.

4. Rule of Historical Background

The history of the life and society of the Jews in biblical times is essential to understanding. Our modern life and society places different meanings and context on words and concepts and must not be used to understand anything of ancient history.

5. Rule of Logic

Logic in interpretation must be everywhere assumed. Jesus used logic many times in exposing and refuting his adversaries. When an idea or premise is followed to its logical conclusion and that conclusion is ridiculous, or outright contradictory to well known fact, that idea or premise must be assumed to be false.

6. Rule of Precedent

We must not violate the known usage or definition of words used in the Bible by inventing new ones for which there is no precedent.

7. Rule of Unity

When a document is comprised of several parts, they should be read together as one.

8. Rule of Inference

Inference is a fact logically implied from another fact, a process of reasoning. It is a logical derivation from a given premise. Jesus proved the resurrection of the dead to the unbelieving Sadducees by this rule (Matt. 22:31, 32).

9. Rule of Consistency

Consistency is a unity of meaning and definition throughout the entirety of a document. The whole Bible is a context.

Satan's argument structure

The first item from Scripture is found in an analysis of Satan's temptation of Eve through the serpent in the Garden of Eden in Genesis 3.

Genesis 3:1-5 (NASB) *"1 Now the serpent*

was more crafty than any beast of the field which the Lord God had made. And he said to the woman, "Indeed, has God said, 'You shall not eat from any tree of the garden'?" [2] The woman said to the serpent, "From the fruit of the trees of the garden we may eat; [3] but from the fruit of the tree which is in the middle of the garden, God has said, 'You shall not eat from it or touch it, or you will die.'" [4] The serpent said to the woman, "You surely will not die! [5] For God knows that in the day you eat from it your eyes will be opened, and you will be like God, knowing good and evil." "

Let's focus on what the serpent stated and understand what the intent of the statements are. The first thing the serpent said was a twist on what God had said to Adam in Genesis 2:16-17, that he could eat from any tree freely with the exception of the tree of the knowledge of good and evil. The serpent stated things differently than God had stated, and in such a way that it cast doubt on the validity and credibility of God's word in addition to being the opposite of what God had said. The second thing the serpent stated was in response to part of what Eve replied with. Eve correctly stated that eating from that one tree would result in death, and added the idea of "touch" to it. Here the serpent stated the exact opposite of what God had said – God said they would surely die, the serpent stated that they would NOT die. And then the third thing the serpent stated was about something that God had not stated at all, neither positively or negatively – "you will be like God."

So, the 3 things stated by the serpent were, 1) casting doubt on the truth and validity of what God actually stated, 2) the exact opposite of what God had already stated, and 3) his own idea - something that God had not said anything about at all. Unfortunately, Satan has been successful in using this strategy on people ever since this situation in the Garden of Eden. There are other strategies that have been used against people that have also been successful, but for our purposes this strategy is sufficient. I have found the exact argument structure of this satanic strategy in many modern theological writings (modern meaning since the AD 1500's).

False teachers from among the saints

The second thing I found is in 2 Peter.

2 Peter 2:1 (NASB) *"¹ But false prophets also arose among the people, just as there will also be false teachers among you, who will secretly introduce destructive heresies, even denying the Master who bought them, bringing swift destruction upon themselves."*

Peter was writing (2 Peter 1:1b) (NASB) *"... To those who have received a faith of the same kind as ours, by the righteousness of our God and Savior, Jesus Christ."* That is a complicated way of identifying saints, or born-again believers. At the beginning of chapter 2, Peter identifies that false teachers will arise among the saints. The obvious understanding of this is that just because someone has been to seminary, or has a handful of Ph. D's in theology, does not mean they cannot be deceived and teach something false. This can run the gamut from minor twists on God's word within predominately Christian denominations, to major twists on God's word within denominations, to what we call major cults such as Mormonism, and Jehovah's Witnesses. The more subtle twists can cause a lot of spiritual damage just because the twists sound good and no one really checks things out with what is actually written as the Berean's did in Acts 17. Here they listened to Paul and then went to the Scriptures to make sure that what Paul had said is really true.

Pardon me, but I will never knowingly trust any so-called theologian who either calls Jesus (or God) a liar, or mimics Satan's ways, or consistently breaks the basic concepts outlined here.

God's curse on modifying His word

The third item from Scripture is what I have labeled "God's curse on modifying His word." There are five passages throughout Scripture that identify this curse. These are: Deuteronomy 4:2, 18:18-22; Proverbs 30:6; Jeremiah 26:2; Revelation 22:18-19. When you read these five passages there is a consistency of things that show us that we are to pay attention to all of God's word, we are not to leave out or omit any of God's word, and we are not to add anything to God's word. (Note that the serpent violated all three of these issues.)

In Deuteronomy 18:19, God specifically addresses the "listener" to God's word through His prophet. The prophet must relay all of the words God wants him to speak, and the listener must also pay attention to all of God's words through the prophet. If the listener does not do this, then "*I will require it of him.*" The use of that phrase in ancient Hebrew basically means that God will make an inquisition of that listener. I don't know about you, but I certainly don't want to be the focus of God's inquisition – God is the judge, prosecutor, and executioner – that's a lose-lose-lose situation for the listener.

Basics summary

To summarize these four concepts, we must be aware of Satan's schemes to deceive us (Ephesians 6). The 9 Rules of Interpretation should be considered as basic reading fundamentals. No matter what we read or hear, we must never violate simple reading fundamentals, God doesn't. We must be mindful that educated Christians can be deceived and provide false teaching, and finally, we do not have God's permission, nor instruction, to make modifications to His word. These four concepts are the most basic things we must know in order to understand God's word. Please be careful with the third issue – most of the educated Christians I have heard teaching, are very desirous to be correct. Sometimes preachers and teachers get "fumble-tongued" and make clumsy statements that can be misleading. We must be careful to take this very human stumbling for just what it really is and not take it to an extreme. But at the same time, be aware that there might be something behind it.

An excellent example of modern theologians mimicking Satan's argument structure in Genesis chapter 3 can be found in Calvin's Commentary for Matthew 8:12. Here, Calvin disparages Jesus use of the label "sons of the kingdom" (NASB) effectively calling Jesus a liar, and uses the exact same argument structure as used by the serpent. Personally, I have a difficult time trusting anyone, particularly theologians, who use Satan's argument structure against what the Holy Spirit has inspired to be written. Theologians do not know better than God the Holy Spirit what spiritual truth really is. And theologians are not ordained to correct what they perceive to be God's "mistakes."

Please evaluate these four issues I have just

described and realize that, for the most part, I am using God's words of instruction and insight to understand God's word. There are also some things that come in handy considering that I speak English and not Greek or Hebrew in which the original word of God was spoken and written. I, as well as you, need assistance in getting to the basic meaning of the words that the Holy Spirit inspired to be spoken and written. I am grateful to the translators that have provided us with over 35 translations of the original languages of Scripture in modern times. I believe that when Peter identified false teachers rising from among the saints, that it covers the entire gamut of people involved with God's word, the scribes who copied, the translators, the professors, the teachers, the preachers, the Sunday School teacher, even our parents. We are to honor our parents, but that does not mean that everything they think the Bible is supposed to say is actually written there. Each and every one of us, individually, are responsible for what we believe. It is our responsibility to make certain as to the source and authority of what we believe.

I seriously doubt that God is going to hold someone responsible for not knowing the original Greek and Hebrew texts when they have no means of learning those languages and probably do not have any inclination to do so. Most Christians must depend on biblically educated Christians to provide training and explanations of what is actually written in Scripture. There are many things in the Bible that are very simple and easy to understand, such as "all have sinned and fallen short of the glory of God." We cannot attain to the glory of God, He is beyond our grasp based on our own strength. Another is, "... that whosoever believes on him will not perish, but have eternal life." When King James commissioned the Bible translation we know as the KJV, he wanted a translation of the Bible so that the common ordinary person walking the streets of London would be able to find salvation just by reading it. ("The Translators To The Reader," available online.)

The best way of understanding another person is to find out from them the best way to do that. This is especially true when trying to understand God, whose ways are more excellent than our ways, and who is infinite while we are finite. The four concepts described above provide the basics of understanding the Bible.

Context is everything

This is a repeat with more detail than listed under the Rule of Context in the "9 Rules of Interpretation" above. This is one of the most violated concepts of interpretation and understanding. You have probably heard the old adage, "Context is everything." Merriam-Webster defines context as: *"1 : the parts of a discourse that surround a word or passage and can throw light on its meaning. 2 : the interrelated conditions in which something exists or occurs :* " Evaluating the context of a word, phrase, or sentence can help keep things in their proper perspective and relationship and aid in understanding what we read. For instance, have you ever tried to identify the general, overall context of the Bible? Consider this: The overall context of the Bible is simply the conflict between good and evil. In Genesis chapters one and two, we find God setting up the environment and situation for the battle, chapter three describes the beginning of the battle, and the book of Revelation shows us the end of evil and all those who choose that path in life. In between the beginning and the end are descriptions of various skirmishes and how God made provision for people to be on the winning side. Simplistic, yes, but very characteristic of how God has chosen to communicate with us. Some things are more complicated, but Jesus, in John 14 and 16, tells us that the Holy Spirit will guide us and teach us. We just need to be willing to listen and learn.

We frequently talk about "taking something out of context." That concept falls directly under God's curse on modifying His word, specifically the aspect of leaving out or omitting some of His word. Taking something out of context is just not taking into account all the words that are legitimately part of the whole picture that is presented in the words of the context.

Deception In Gospel Presentation

Sometimes, deception comes when teaching accomplishes two of the aspects of God's curse on modifying His word and thereby changing the meaning of the original context. This is done by simply substituting a different word for a word that is actually written in the Bible. Some religious philosophies will take Romans 8:29, omit "foreknew" and add in "foreordained." Those two words have very different meanings that are not in the least similar. "Foreordain" means to "appoint or decree (something) beforehand," while "foreknow" means to "be aware (of an event) beforehand." Those who swap these words would require a journalist to be guilty of causing an accident on the highway just because they publish information about it. Unfortunately, Satan is successful in deceiving people by doing this kind of thing.

Deception in understanding the results of the Gospel

Most religious groups would agree that one of the basic concepts of salvation hinges on believing in Jesus as written in the following verses:

John 3:16 (NASB) *"16 "For God so loved the world, that He gave His only begotten Son, that whoever believes in Him shall not perish, but have eternal life.""*

John 6:35 (NASB) *"35 Jesus said to them, "I am the bread of life; he who comes to Me will not hunger, and he who believes in Me will never thirst."*

Acts 16:31 (NASB) *"31 They said, "Believe in the Lord Jesus, and you will be saved, you and your household." "*

Romans 10:9-10 (NASB) *"9 that if you confess with your mouth Jesus as Lord, and believe in your heart that God raised Him from the dead, you will be saved; 10 for with the heart a person believes, resulting in righteousness, and with the mouth he confesses, resulting in salvation."*

There is a significant discrepancy in what all may result in that event of believing. Most groups identify that this belief results in the indwelling of the Holy Spirit in the person believing. This is some-times referred to as "being sealed by the Holy Spirit for salvation and/or redemption."

2 Corinthians 1:21-22 (NASB) *"²¹ Now He who establishes us with you in Christ and anointed us is God, ²² who also sealed us and gave us the Spirit in our hearts as a pledge."*

Ephesians 1:13-14 (NASB) *"¹³ In Him, you also, after listening to the message of truth, the gospel of your salvation—having also believed, you were sealed in Him with the Holy Spirit of promise, ¹⁴ who is given as a pledge of our inheritance, with a view to the redemption of God's own possession, to the praise of His glory."*

Ephesians 4:30 (NASB) *"³⁰ Do not grieve the Holy Spirit of God, by whom you were sealed for the day of redemption."*

Pentecost

Then comes the question of what all goes on relative to the day of Pentecost, and is it relevant to Christians today, and if so, when does it become part of a Christian's life? There are a few various philosophies about all this. One philosophy thinks that everything happens at the new birth, the in-dwelling of the Holy Spirit, the power of the Holy Spirit, gifts, etc. Some that follow this line of thought also believe that the disciples were born-again on the day of Pentecost, the 50th day after Christ's resurrection. I heard one such thought process from a preacher who accurately quoted Acts 1:8,

Acts 1:8 (NASB) *"⁸ but you will receive power*

when the Holy Spirit has come upon you; and you shall be My witnesses both in Jerusalem, and in all Judea and Samaria, and even to the remotest part of the earth."

...and seconds later misquoted it, leaving out a very important part of the verse, and totally ignoring other verses. The re-quote was "you will receive power when the Holy Spirit comes." This misquote was then used as the launch point for his thought that we get everything when the Holy Spirit comes. In the Greek, there are actual words for the translation of "has come upon you," and these were the words that were left out. There is a difference between "the Holy Spirit comes," and "the Holy Spirit has come upon you." The implication of this misquote was that the Holy Spirit comes "into" you instead "upon" you. This is an obvious case of both leaving out some of God's word (omission) and then adding something into God's word because of his implication based on the conclusions that were drawn from his misquote. There is a consistency between the concepts of "clothed" and "come upon," and even the KJV "endued." We need to pay attention to all these items. We'll get deeper into this.

Luke 24:49 (NASB) *"49 And behold, I am sending forth the promise of My Father upon you; but you are to stay in the city until you are clothed with power from on high."*

Deception In Gospel Presentation

Here Luke records what Jesus says is to take place on Pentecost as being "<u>clothed</u> with <u>power</u> from on high." It may seem like a silly point, but clothing is something placed on the outside of the body, not the inside. Why would Jesus use this terminology if something different was meant such as the Holy Spirit coming inside you? Other verses identify that the Holy Spirit lives within us and that the Holy Spirit is life. And compare this to Acts 1:8, "the Holy Spirit has come upon you." Luke did not quote Jesus as stating that they were to wait for the indwelling of the Holy Spirit for eternal life, but for the power of the Holy Spirit that will "clothe" us. God is not a God of chaos or confusion. Munging differing terms and treating them as if they were one and the same thing is chaos.

John 20:22 (NASB) "*²² And when He had said this, He breathed on them and *said to them, "<u>Receive</u> the Holy Spirit."*

Here, the statement in the Greek is in an imperative-present-continuing form. This simply means that right there, right then, they received the Holy Spirit who continued with them. This situation is key to understanding the difference between the new-birth and what took place on Pentecost. What Jesus stated took place in the evening of His resurrection day, i.e., the second day of His resurrection according to the way the Jews marked their days (begins at evening and ends at the next evening, not like our modern midnight to midnight). This was when the disciples were sealed with the Holy Spirit for salvation, eternal life and redemption, not on Pentecost. There is a difference between the indwelling of the Holy Spirit for salvation (eternal life) and receiving power by the Holy Spirit coming upon us. The disciples really did have two different encounters with the Holy Spirit. Each encounter was for a different purpose. If you have to, go back and read the section on what I labeled "God's curse on modifying His word." When theologians leave out entire verses and misquote others, so it fits their own ideas (or Satan's deception), what they teach is false. We do not have God's permission, nor instruction to leave out any of His word. It all fits together, we are not to "pick-and-choose" what parts or phrases of God's word to use for our theological beliefs and re-mold the original meanings of words for our convenience and Satan's deception.

If Jesus spoke the words for it to happen when He spoke them and that it would continue, then that is what happened. I have read some commentaries that stated the words Jesus spoke were only prophetic and did not apply in the situation they were spoken in, or the words were only a preparation for a future time. That philosophy effectively makes Jesus a liar based on the words, and the form of the words actually inspired by the Holy Spirit to be recorded for us.

Deception In Gospel Presentation

There is some small symbolism associated with Jesus breathing on each of his disciples that evening of his resurrection. This is simply that Jesus, because of his resurrection, was the firstborn from death (Rev. 1:5; Col. 1:18), and Rom. 8:29 tells us that Jesus is to be the firstborn among many brethren. When Jesus breathed on the disciples that first evening, it was symbolical of the scene in Genesis when God breathed into Adam, and he became a living soul. The disciples became eternal living souls when Jesus breathed on them, and they also became the first of those many brethren.

Here's another weird angle to the false teaching surrounding John 20:22 and Pentecost. If what Jesus said did not happen when he spoke it, but it was only 'prophetic,' and the disciples were not born-again until many days later, what would have been the result if one of them died before Pentecost? They would have gone to hell instead of heaven because they would not have yet received the indwelling of the Holy Spirit. That would also mean that when you believed on Jesus that you did not receive it until many days later – and if you had died in the meantime, then you would have gone to hell also...

Every satanic twist I've read like this has either left out John 20:22 or twisted it's meaning, and if Luke 24:49 or Acts 1:8 is mentioned, it is given a different meaning than the original words. And typically, the words "power," "upon" and "indwelling" are treated as though they were one and the same word. I really *do not believe* that the Holy Spirit messed it up and these theologians are required to correct God.

"Indwelling" and "clothed" are not the same concept. Sealed by the Holy Spirit for salvation/ redemption, is not the same concept as being baptized in the Holy Spirit/receiving power (as was stated by John the Baptist in Matthew 3:11, Mark 1:8, Luke 3:16 and Peter in Acts 10 and 11). Jesus, in John chapters 14 to 16, describes a coming of the Holy Spirit as one who comes <u>alongside</u> to help. "<u>Alongside</u>" is not the same concept as "indwelling." God is NOT a God of chaos or confusion.

Theologians brutalize the Scriptures when they simply slap together words with different meanings, and treat them as one and the same thing, or leave out words, or substitute other meanings. That is definitely a situation of failure to pay attention to ALL God's words, and in many cases is a deliberate attempt to leave out words that do not fit what the theologian wants either because of fleshly desires or satanic deception. And please note, sometimes a theologian may teach something they have been taught by another theologian who is the one who has been deceived. The first theologian in this situation may not have figured out what is really going on, and unfortunately, is being set up for further deception. Play like a Berean and check it out (Acts 17).

But there is one other thing. Why does the New Testament have so many references to being "filled" with the Spirit? Think about something here – what does it mean to be "filled?" We read into the Scriptures things from our own culture and word use and mannerisms. The Greek word means:

(CG-ED) "πληρόω *fulfill, make come true, bring about (of Scripture); fill, make full; bring to* completion*; complete, accomplish, finish; make fully known, proclaim fully*"

When we think of "filled" in our American culture, we typically think of putting something in a container until there is no more room left. That is not the basic concept involved in the word in Greek. Our culture's "filled" has no concept of "completion." This word is also used in the New Testament to indicate the "completion" of, or "fulfillment" of Old Testament scripture. The "container" concept that we have really does NOT fit the meaning of the word in Greek. I heard one theologian state that we need to keep being "filled" because we "leak." Only containers can leak. The point of being "filled" with the Spirit is for completion, to "fill in" the places where we lack, to bring us to a point of "full" maturity in our relation to God in any and every area of our life. Our relation to God is to be on the basis of faith and the work of the Spirit in our lives, not on the basis of faith and the strength of the flesh and the contrivances and ingenuity of our minds. The concept of "completion" and "fulfillment" matches up perfectly with the parakleetos, coming alongside to help.

James 1:4 (NASB) *"4 And let endurance have its perfect result, so that you may be perfect and complete, lacking in nothing."*

Endurance (patience) is to "reach its end" and "be complete and entire," lacking in nothing. It is a process to get all aspects of our life aligned with God's personality and character. The Holy Spirit is "in" us and "beside" us, getting us to that completion.

The Christian life is not a bed of rose petals...

John 16:33 (NASB) *"33 "These things I have spoken to you, so that in Me you may have peace. In the world you have tribulation, but take courage; I have overcome the world.""*

Having salvation in Jesus does not eliminate life's problems and trials. With Christ in our hearts because of the indwelling of the Holy Spirit, we do not have to struggle and endure life's problems alone. Before we had salvation, we had to struggle with life alone. Yes, there are usually other people to lend their sympathy, friends and family, but within the hearts of unbelievers, it is just themselves. The born-again believer has God to lean on, and with the baptism in the Holy Spirit, He is there alongside you to help, strengthen, and encourage you, Prayer is real, the guidance of the Holy Spirit is real. Life's problems are real.

Many verses indicate that the Christian life involves suffering. Take the time to read them in your favorite translation: Matthew 5:10-12; Luke 14:27; Romans 5:3-5, 8:35; 2 Corinthians 1:3-4, 4:8-10, 17; Galatians 6:2; Colossians 1:24; Philippians 3:10; 2 Timothy 3:12; Hebrews 2:10; James 1:2-4, 12; 1 Peter 1:6-7, 2:19-21, 3:14, 4:1, 5:10; Psalms 34:19, 119:71. That is over 20 references to suffering taking place in our lives. The life of Joseph is documented in Genesis 40 to 50. At one point, Joseph interpreted two dreams that Pharaoh had regarding seven years of plenty followed by seven years of famine. One of Joseph's statements was that if God said it twice, He would surely bring it to pass. Here we have over 20 references to suffering in life when we follow God. Guess what? It's gonna happen!

Some will complain that a "loving God" would not permit bad or evil things to happen. This kind of complaint fails to take into account the fact that every action and/or decision has its consequences. Sin has it's consequences. Believing in Jesus for salvation has its consequences. When we make a bad or evil decision, God is not going to stop the consequences from taking place, we have made the choice, and God will leave us to our own consequences (See Romans chapter 1). God will make the effort to persuade His truly born-again children to make a decision for righteousness in every situation, instead of for fleshly lust or evil, but God does not exercise power over those made in His image and likeness. (See Appendix A: God and Control)

This even applies to the fact that death is a part of life. Hebrews 9:27 tells us that we are destined to die once and then face judgment. Eventually, we will all die (or be taken at the Rapture), that is just part of life. Living has its consequences. We should have sorrow when a loved one passes, but to complain to God and blame Him when our 90+-year-old loved one passes is either idolatry of that loved one or extreme selfishness (desire for fleshly lust sanctification), or both. We have the initiative to make a decision for what is righteous (Luke 12:57), we also have the initiative to do things that are bad for our spiritual and/or physical health and suffer the consequences. When you love someone, you only want the best for them; however, love does not control, neither can love prevent others from making bad decisions, and love does not prevent consequences. If love did any or all those types of things, it would not be true love, it would be oppression, it would have to exercise power over another, which is satanic. (See Luke 12:57 and Acts 10:38 below.)

And then there's the situation of all the unbelievers (and yourself before salvation) sins which have a spiritual effect on our entire physical and spiritual environment. Sin compounded upon sin, and we wonder why things go wrong...

Christian Antichrists

That title sounds like a contradiction in terms, but it does accurately label a popular modern movement. Before I present some of the details of this movement, let me identify a caveat. The points of this movement will be presented in what some would call an extreme, but I'm doing that just for the sake of simplicity. The individual members of the movement may not believe any one point to its extreme, nor will any one member necessarily believe each and every point of the movement. There is a variability of belief and involvement of each member.

This movement is probably best known by the label "Word of Faith," (WF). This is a movement as opposed to a denomination. The first belief we will discuss is their idea that they will become God. This comes from the KJV in Philippians 2:5-8, specifically the phrase "thought it not robbery to be equal to God" out of context. The thought which follows that phrase indicates that Jesus made that "not robbery" phrase powerless or void according to the Greek meanings of words in the KJV phrase "made himself of no reputation.". The beginning of that passage says that we are to have the same mind as was in

Christ, but the WF takes the concept of "equal to God" out of context and ignores the "made powerless" concept which immediately follows. In many of the modern translations, the wording of "emptied himself" or "made void" is used for that Greek word. The basic meaning of the word means:

(Greek-English Lexicon, The - by Louw & Nida) *"76.27 κενόω (1) to take away the power or significance of something - to cause to lose power, to cause to be emptied of power, to make powerless."*

This can be better understood by evaluating the use of this word "κενόω" in the other verses in the New Testament: Romans 4:14; 1 Corinthians 1:17; 1 Corinthians 9:15, 2 Corinthians 9:3.

A simple concept that also refutes the idea of Christians becoming God is that God is "self-existent," which comes from God's description of himself to Moses: "I AM THAT I AM." Christians are initially created beings and therefore can never become "self-existent."

Revelation 21:7 (NASB) *"⁷ He who overcomes will inherit these things, and I will be his God and he will be My son."*

Verse 5 of this chapter identifies the speaker as the one who sits on the throne, obviously God the Father. The one who overcomes is a reference to what Jesus states to the Churches in chapters 2 and 3, the born again believer who faces sin and is a conquerer (overcomer). Here it is stated that our ongoing relationship to God (Father, Son, Spirit) will always be as a child. It is difficult, if not impossible, to reconcile always being a child with becoming God.

And then there is the end of Isaiah 43:10, "... Before Me there was no God formed, And there will be none after Me." No, Christians will not become God.

Another twisted idea they have is that since we are to be "Christ-like" we will be "equal" to God. They twist the meaning of "like" to mean "equal" when the words in Greek do not mean the same thing.

Like: (CWSB Dictionary) *"3667. ὁμοίωμα homoíōma; gen. homoiṓmatos, neut. noun from homoióō (G3666), to make like. Likeness, shape, similitude, resemblance. It is important to realize that the resemblance signified by homoíōma in no way implies that one of the objects in question has been derived from the other. In the same way two men may resemble one another even though they are in no way related to one another."*

Equal: (CWSB Dictionary) *"2470. ἴσος ísos; fem. ísē, neut. íson, adj. Equal, alike in quantity, quality, dignity."*

Even in our American English, we have the

words "alike" and "like." Placing the "a" at the beginning of a word makes it mean the opposite of the base word. "Alike" means "equal to," and therefore the base word "like" means "not equal to," "similar, but of lesser quality."

1 Peter 1:3-4 tells us that we are to be partakers in God's nature. This is also used by them to mean that we will become God. And then Psalm 82:6 "ye are gods" has been given a different meaning than what the context indicates. The context of Psalm 82:6 is referring to the rulers and magistrates of the people who are to be handing out judgments as God's representatives, not that those people are equal to God (they die like men). When Jesus used this in John 10, he was not calling them "divine" as WF implies, he was pointing out their responsibility that they were misusing.

Hebrews 1:3 contains the phrase "the express image of his person," which is interpreted to mean "the exact (equal) likeness" but they leave out the rest. The Greek simply states that he (Jesus) is the assurance or substance of his (God the Father's) character.

Another twisted idea they have is from Romans 10:8-10, specifically the idea that the word of faith is in our mouth, and we are to speak it. The WF interprets that to mean that we will speak things into existence (like worlds and galaxies). The problem is that verses 9-10 define that word of spoken faith as our belief on Jesus for salvation.

The WF also takes verses such as Genesis 1:3, 6, 9, where God spoke things into existence to mean we will do the same. We will never do that. God can do that because he is existence itself ("I AM"), and we are not "self-existent."

Matthew 10:24-25 (NASB) *"24 "A disciple is not above his teacher, nor a slave above his master. 25 It is enough for the disciple that he become like his teacher, and the slave like his master. If they have called the head of the house Beelzebul, how much more will they malign the members of his household!""*

Here also,, the WF again applies a different concept to the words written than what they really mean. If you study the meanings of "like" and "equal" in Greek lexicons, they mean different things (See definitions above). Here in Matthew they interpret "like" to mean "equal."

The "Mona Lisa" is a resemblance to a woman but is not the woman herself.

The WF really began back in Genesis 3 with the phrase "you will be like God" which the serpent used in the temptation of Eve. Satan has continued to use that idea and take things out of context and substitute different meanings of words to support the false concept "you will become God".

Deceptions in how the new birth takes place

Believe versus work

When the words "believe" and "faith" are examined closely in the Greek, it becomes very evident that both of those words mean "to have a firm persuasion. "Believe" is the verb derived from the noun "faith," and "faith" is derived from the Greek word for "persuade." It is also interesting that faith and believe are in the passive voice in the Greek, which means these items do not, in and of themselves, initiate or take action. "Faith" and "believe" are in the passive voice "branch" of persuade. The active voice branch of persuade are the words trustworthy and trust. The active voice means that the concept represented by the word(s) initiates action.

The beginning of Romans 4:5 is: *"But to him who does not work but believes..."* We need to pay attention to words here. What does the word "but" mean? Many will reply that "but" is a conjunction. "Conjunction" is the word's grammatical classification, not it's meaning. The word "but" is an adversarial term that means that what follows is adverse to what came before (either a word or phrase or concept). Romans 4:5 simply tells us that "believes" is adverse to work. Some religious philosophies teach that "believe" is work, the opposite of what is actually written in God's word here in Romans 4:5. This false teaching mimics the second characteristic of Satan's argument structure as identified above.

Believing is not work according to what is actually written in Scripture. And the meanings of "faith" and "believe" are based on the word "persuade." Over 20 times, Paul uses a form of the word persuade to describe his intent and method of Gospel presentation to both Jew and Gentile. It would seem drastically out of God's character for Paul to use persuasion and was inspired by the Holy Spirit to write most of the New Testament, and then have God, the Holy Spirit, use force in some manner to make people born-again. God does not change. God uses persuasion instead of force on those created in His own image and likeness.

Even in the book of Jonah, God controlled the storm, fish, plant, worm, and wind, but not Jonah. Those other things are not created in His image and likeness. The situation comes to a critical point of ridiculousness when you consider that if God created people as controlled beings, and they are made in His image and likeness, then God himself is a controlled being. At that point, one must ask, "Who or what then controls God?" Obviously, no one controls God; therefore the premise of "people are controlled by God" is false.

We have the choice

Luke 12:57 (NASB) "*57* *"And why do you not*

even on your own <u>initiative judge</u> what is <u>right</u>?"

When the Greek for this verse is evaluated, it becomes obvious that the word "judge" means "make a decision" and the word "right" is most frequently translated as "righteous." "Initiative" means "the ability to assess and initiate things independently: the power or opportunity to act or take charge before others do." Plugging those meanings into the statement, it reads:

"And why do you not even on your own ability to assess and initiate things independently, make a decision for what is righteous?" Jesus is stating in so many words that people have the ability for making a decision for what is righteous. It is up to us to act on that initiative or not. The idea that salvation must be forced on people also carries the idea that it must be forced on people because they cannot make a decision for righteousness or God. That teaching is the opposite of what Jesus stated here in Luke 12:57. Keep in mind that Jesus is the Son of God - one should expect that God would know if people really had that ability or not. And, if they really do have that ability as Jesus is stating, then that philosophy is really calling Jesus a liar.

Acts 10:38 (NASB) *"³⁸ You know of Jesus of Nazareth, how God anointed Him with the Holy Spirit and with power, and how He went about doing good and healing all who were <u>oppressed</u> by the devil, for God was with Him."*

Deception In Gospel Presentation

In this short summary of the ministry of Jesus when he was here on Earth, we also find that oppression is by (or from) the devil. The word "oppress" simply means, "to exercise power over another." Now comes the shocking part... Those religious philosophies that teach the Holy Spirit forces salvation on people, are committing blasphemy of the Holy Spirit by simply taking something obviously satanic, according to what is actually written in Scripture, and directly applying it to the Holy Spirit. Some groups think that blasphemy of the Holy Spirit cannot be committed today, basically because Jesus is no longer here on Earth. This is derived from adding (reading into) to the Scriptures. When Jesus was accused of casting out demons by Beelzebub, these theologians assume that because they are identifying the power or authority of Jesus to the devil, that they really meant the Holy Spirit. It is actually more complicated and convoluted than that, but I'm trying to use simple terms here. They assume then that the only way to commit blasphemy of the Holy Spirit is to make that, and only that, specific accusation to Jesus. The problem is that the words were directed to Jesus and not the Holy Spirit. And blasphemy, and even speaking something against anyone (for that matter) is easier to do when the person is not present. See Matt 12:31, 32; Mark 3:28-30; Luke 12:10 and the context of these verses.

In Matthew 12:32, Jesus used a word in reference to both the Son and the Spirit that is translated "against." The meaning in the Greek is simply "down, against." That can cover a broad range of speech, not just the narrow specific issue some take, that I have just identified.

The Holy Spirit persuades us to believe in Jesus for salvation, and since God does not change, our on-going relationship with God is handled on the same basis of persuasion.

Romans 2:8 (NASB) *"8 but to those who are selfishly ambitious and <u>do not obey</u> the truth, but <u>obey</u> unrighteousness, wrath and indignation."*

In my electronic Bible, I have several translations which can display the Strong's numbers of the words. When I read this verse, I noticed that "obey" is used twice, but each use has a different Strong's number. When I checked this out, I found that both places where "obey" is used it is based on the word "persuade." In English, we have the words "typical" and "atypical." Adding the letter "a" in front changes the meaning of the word to the opposite of the base word. So, "typical" would mean the usual kind of thing, and "atypical" would mean the unusual kind of thing.. Greek has many words that can be treated in the identical manner, and this is what is being done with the word "persuade" in Romans 2:8. Along with the endings of the Greek words (which identifies the case, tense, gender and other grammatical things),

Romans 2:8 would read: "but to those who are self-ishly ambitious and <u>refuse to be persuaded</u> to the truth, but <u>are persuaded</u> to unrighteousness, wrath and indignation." People's choice of righteousness or unrighteousness is based on persuasion, not force.

Luke 22:25-26 (NASB) "*25 And He said to them, "The kings of the Gentiles lord it over them; and those who have authority over them are called 'Benefactors.' 26 <u>But it is not this way with you</u>, but the one who is the greatest among you must become like the youngest, and the leader like the servant." "*

Here, Jesus is talking to his disciples and making a contrast between Satan's way of running the world system versus the kingdom of God. The phrase "lord it over them" means the identical thing as "oppressed" in Acts 10:38. "Lording it over them" is Satan's way of controlling people, exercising power over them. Contrast that with the kingdom of God where the leader is a servant. This is just another word picture that identifies the difference between the satanically twisted religious philosophies, and the truth of God's word. God does not force salvation on anyone, that behavior is identified at least two times within Scripture as being satanic, or from the devil. Again, God does not change, nor is he a God of chaos or confusion, and he is against leaving out, or adding to, any of his word.

The religious philosophies that teach the Holy Spirit must force salvation on people also frequently teach that each of us is individually and totally responsible for our own sins. There are many convoluted ways of trying to explain away this obvious contradiction. The contradiction is that if God must force salvation on people, behind that is God making the choice of who is going to heaven and who is going to hell, If God picks the ones in both situations, then God would also be responsible for the sin of the people who pay the penalty by being in hell for eternity because He is withholding forgiveness from them. This contradiction only exists because of the satanically twisted beliefs that both, God picks people for heaven or hell, and must force salvation on those he has picked for heaven (since they allegedly cannot choose righteousness or God). If you are confused about the last few statements, welcome to the club.

The contradiction simply does not exist if people really do have the ability on their own initiative to make a decision for righteousness or God, as Jesus stated (quoted above in Luke 12:57). People do have the capability of making a decision for what is righteous, and that is why they are completely and totally responsible for their own sins. It really is their own choice.

What about works?

Ephesians 2:8-10 (NASB) *"⁸ For by grace you*

35

*have been saved through faith; and that not of your-
selves, it is the gift of God; ⁹ not as a result of works,
so that no one may boast. ¹⁰ For we are His work-
manship, created in Christ Jesus for good works,
which God prepared beforehand so that we would
walk in them."*

Romans 3:28 (NASB) *"²⁸ For we maintain that
a man is justified by faith apart from works of the
Law."*

2 Timothy 1:8-9 (NASB) *"⁸ Therefore do not be
ashamed of the testimony of our Lord or of me His
prisoner, but join with me in suffering for the gospel
according to the power of God, ⁹ who has saved us
and called us with a holy calling, not according to
our works, but according to His own purpose and
grace which was granted us in Christ Jesus from all
eternity,"*

James 2:14 (NASB) *"¹⁴ What use is it, my
brethren, if someone says he has faith but he has
no works? Can that faith save him?"*

James 2:18 (NASB) *"¹⁸ But someone may well
say, "You have faith and I have works; show me
your faith without the works, and I will show you my
faith by my works." "*

The passages here in Ephesians, Romans,
and 2 Timothy very clearly demonstrate that we
cannot earn or obtain salvation by our own works or
any works of the Law (Old Testament Law given by
God through Moses at Mt. Sinai). Then we slam into

the statements made by James. I've read several dissertations by different theologians who claim that James is saying that our salvation is by a combination of both faith and works. Here we go again with God's curse on modifying His word...

James frames his question in verse 14 with the accusative case form of "works," and responds in verse 18 with "works" in the genitive case form for both uses of "works" in that verse.

The accusative is used to limit the action of a verb as to extent, direction or goal. The accusative measures an idea as to its content, scope, direction.

The genitive is the case of qualification (or limitation) as to kind, and (occasionally) separation.

Let me explain this in simple terms (as simply as I can). The question posed only states the possession of faith, but no works is indicating that faith has no need of works. Works provide no direction or goal that goes along with faith. James' response uses "works" in a qualified sense indicating there is a particular kind or type of works he is meaning. That kind or type of "works" is something that shows or demonstrates that his faith exists.

The posed question may be understood as stating that faith needs no proof of existence, and James replies that his faith is not "earning" his salvation, but is a demonstration that the faith and salvation exists. There is a time sequence of events indicated here. Before we have salvation, we might

get the idea that we could work our way into salvation, but the earlier verses deny that possibility.
When we do find salvation by "faith," then one might
think that any "works" could only apply to an attempt
to "earn" salvation. James is stating that "works" is
the evidence that faith has had God's desired and
intended result, and that has nothing to do with
"earning" any salvation or faith.

Before we are born-again, any works are
worthless, but after the new birth event, works do
have a proper place in the life of a Christian as
evidence that God's salvation now exists in that
person. Many fail to recognize any kind of time sequence of events in their understanding of "works"
and fail to understand that God has previously
identified specific "works" that his children are to be
participating in (Ephesians 2:10 above). The good
works were created beforehand, NOT the person
("we"). There is something that God wants us to do,
to participate in, and it is those things which God
prepared beforehand, "we" are to walk in them.
(How could we "walk in ourselves" if "we" are the
ones created in salvation beforehand? If following
something to its logical conclusion results in something illogical or ridiculous, that means the starting
premise is wrong.).

We must understand that "works" encompasses not only energy and effort, but our behavior, our
mannerisms, what we speak and how we speak it

(Romans 10:10, Matthew 12:34), the expression of our attitudes, and many other aspects of being a person created in God's image and likeness. "Works" also encompasses the gifts of the Spirit, the ministry God invites us to, and what part of the body of Christ we are (Romans 12 and 1 Corinthians 12). This goes along with Romans 8:29 where our being conformed to the image of His son is what was predestined, not whether one goes to heaven or hell as some satanically twisted religious philosophies contend.

Epilogue

Satan's point and purpose for deception in the presentations of the Gospel is to have people killed (or simply die) without salvation, and destroy any possible effectiveness of the Gospel in a person's life if they do find salvation by believing in Jesus. We started off with "9 Rules of Interpretation" which turn out to be simple reading fundamentals. God speaks to us on our level, in our vernacular (method of communication). Then we examined several passages in the Scriptures that clue us into how God wants us to handle His word and how Satan, through the serpent, deceived Eve, and one of the more obvious points of entry of his deception into the Church, false teachers rising from among the saints. Context was discussed and how that can be manipulated to make deception sound like truth. The specific items identified for the results of the new birth, and how the new birth takes place are not intended to be a comprehensive list of all Satan's deceptions, just the most frequently used.

Some of the basics were presented for believing in Jesus for salvation and redemption, and then how deception is implemented when Pentecost is considered. The actual words that were inspired to be written indicate the disciples had two separate encounters with the Holy Spirit, each for a different purpose. The deceptions around this are varied but usually involve ignoring John 20:22, and/or modifying the meanings of the words used there and in Luke 24:49 and Acts 1:8. Since God identifies we are to pay attention to all His words and not leave out any of them, nor add to them, ignoring words and changing the original meaning falls under God's curse. ...Not a place where I want to find myself.

Some people call it "Easy Believe-ism." It basically amounts to deceiving people into thinking that salvation cures and eliminates all possible problems in life. Not true. Over 20 references were provided that suffering is going to happen.

Then we got into how the new birth takes place. We identified that believing is not work as some deceivers teach. The Holy Spirit uses persuasion to get us to change our mind (repentance), and believe in our heart in Jesus. We have the choice based on our own initiative to make a decision for what is righteous.

We also delved into the word "works" and the two different situations and contexts it is used in within the Scriptures. We cannot work to "earn" our salvation, but once the salvation event has taken place by faith, there are "works" which God already prepared for us so that the faith and salvation within us is demonstrated by these "works" to others.

Every deception we believe impedes our relationship to God and diminishes our witness and testimony to others who need salvation. We may not like the terminology, but we are at war for our own salvation and the salvation of others. God provides us with everything that is needed for His victory to be real in our own lives. You would never carry boulders in your backpack while climbing a mountain; the deceptions we believe have the same effect on our spiritual lives. The choice is yours to carry the boulders or dump them.

Appendix A: God and Control

One of the reasons that Satan is so successful in the method I'll be discussing is because of how carelessly we read and how little effort we apply to understanding the words and sentences we read. In Genesis 3, we have recorded the temptation of Eve to sin against God, here's a brief summary. Satan started with casting doubt on what God had said; then, he stated the opposite of what God had said (God: eat that fruit and you will die, versus Satan: you will surely NOT die.); and then he added his opinion in a way that made it sound better than what God had said (you can be your own god, knowing good and evil [knowing good and evil was only a fringe benefit, the real point of the deception was the being your own god part]). Apparently without thinking very much about what was actually stated to her, Eve took the idea of being her own god and "justified" it by taking the attributes of the tree and fruit as "evidence" of the alleged truth of what was said to her. Ergo sin in humanity.

Let's take a look, briefly, at the meaning of "insidious:" "proceeding in a gradual, subtle way, but with harmful effects; treacherous; crafty." Satan has been using the same insidious tactic of deception against all humanity from that time to the present. His success rate is phenomenally high as far as taking people off target by just introducing opinion into the conversation. We will take a look at some examples where at first you may not understand the deception, but with a little thought and paying attention to the things I point out, you will begin to understand a little better how Satan may be deceiving you.

Let's start with the idea that "God is in control." Perform an Internet search with your favorite search engine, looking for the words: "God is in control." You will find more things to read on the first page of the results than you want to spend the time reading, but take a look at least a handful of them and you will see what I mean. One of the titles I found when I went to the actual web page was: "33 Verses about Fear and Anxiety to Remind Us: God is in Control" I read each of those 33 verses, and found that each had something to say about fear, anxiety, worry, etc., but no words used in those references there actually said anything about "God is in control." In each of those verses the things stated are regarding what God does in our heart and mind when we are enduring difficult situations. NONE of those verses indicate that God changes the circumstances, only our heart and mind attitude toward the situation (away from the trauma and toward God and the peace He instills in our hearts and minds).

The deception comes in the title of the article. The first part is true, 33 verses about fear and anxiety", but the part implying that God is in control is not part of any of the verses. People use statements like this with Satan's deceptive opinion added on to avoid having to live by faith because their dependence on God is almost irrelevant since God is supposed to manipulate and control things and themselves anyhow.

In my bible app, I can do complex searches of the Scripture, and identify associations within a range of verses, not just one verse. That permits me to search for word associations within Paul's run-on sentences that span 7-9 verses at times. I can search within Paul's "paragraphs" not just a single verse. I found several verses about God (or Jesus) commanding what we could call "forces of nature," wind, waves, etc., but nothing about changing the circumstances we have to deal with. The only "circumstantial" things that I have found in Scripture that change are the removal of demons in the name of Jesus and God providing a means of escape from a situation under some circumstances. We'll find more detail on this as we go through this discussion.

Let's examine some of the verses about fear and worry and anxiety to see what they really mean.

Psalm 34:7 tells us He will rescue us – rescue means to draw off or out. That is regarding us, not the circumstances or the situation (see 1 Cor. 10:13 below).

Psalm 14:19, Isaiah 33:22, Isaiah 35:4 tell us that He will save us – "save" means to deliver. Again, that is regarding us, the situation could continue on.

Deception In Gospel Presentation

Psalm 55:22 tells us He will sustain us and we will not be shaken – sustain means to contain, shaken means to totter (we will be stable). Us, not the situation.

Deut. 31:6 – he will never leave us or forsake us – This does dot state that God manipulates the circumstances, only that He will be with us, in and/or through the situation.

Deut 3:22 says that God is the one fighting for you – God may fight, but this provides no description of what "fighting" really is and what all is involved. This lends no evidence to either side of the situation.

Zeph. 3:17 calls God a "victorious warrior." That phrase simply means "to deliver mightily." That is the same as "rescue" above – to draw off or out.

Psalm 91:16 – God will let him see His salvation – the root for "salvation" means "to deliver," the person, not to change the situation.

2 Cor. 5:14 – the love of Christ controls us – the word "controls" means "to hold together." The love of Christ holds us together. Nothing here about manipulating circumstances.

Prov. 29:25 – whoever trusts in the Lord is kept safe. Nothing here about what, if anything, God does to the circumstances.

Similar kinds of statements are found in all the other references regarding fear, worry, anxiety.

All these statements focus on the believer in God, not the circumstances. The believer in God is the item that is changed, from worry etc., to stability and peace in their heart and mind because of the presence of the Holy Spirit in our lives..

Ge 43:31, Ge 45:1, Ex 32:25, 2Sa 8:1, 2Ch 17:5, Es 5:10, Pr 25:28, Ec 2:19, Da 11:43, Ac 5:4, Ac 24:25, Ac 27:16, 1Co 7:5, 1Co 7:9, 1Co 9:25, 2Co 5:14, Ga 5:23, 1Th 5:6, 1Th 5:8, 1Ti 3:4, 2Ti 3:3, Tit 1:8, Jas 1:26, 2Pe 1:6 are verses that use some form of the word "control." None of them identify God doing any control over anything. These all identify people being in control of something or self-control. Acts 10:38 tells us that Jesus healed and delivered all who were oppressed by the devil. The word "oppressed" means "to exercise power over another." Only the devil is identified in Scripture as exercising power over another (control) person, God is never identified as exercising power over those created in His image and likeness. The dictionary definition of control is: "the power to influence to direct people's behavior or the course of events." According to this definition, the only "control" God has on His people is influence, usually identified as persuasion. The only "control" God gives to people, regarding people, is "self-control." None of the verses regarding fear, anxiety, worry indicate anything about changing the course of the situation one might find themselves in.

Deception In Gospel Presentation

We can take 1 Cor. 10:13 in principle for this issue of control. No temptation will be greater than what we are able to handle, and if it is greater, God provides a way of escape so that we do not succumb to the situation. If the fear, anxiety, worry is too great for us to handle, God provides a means for us to vacate the situation, he "opens a door", so to speak, but we need to go through it. We are no longer part of the situation which might actually continue on without us. The real point is God's work on our hearts and minds, not the circumstances.

Another issue is identifiable in the typical Calvinist concept that people cannot, are not capable or able, to choose righteousness or Jesus. This leads to the blasphemy of the Holy Spirit concept of salvation being forced on people by the Holy Spirit so they can be given faith so they can believe on Jesus. A typical statement goes like this:

"The doctrine of Total Depravity is derived from scriptures that reveal human character: Man's heart is evil (Mark 7:21-23) and sick (Jer. 17:9). Man is a slave of sin (Rom. 6:20). He does not seek for God (Rom. 3:10-12). He cannot understand spiritual things (1 Cor. 2:14). He is at enmity with God (Eph. 2:15). And, is by nature a child of wrath (Eph. 2:3). The Calvinist asks the question, "In light of the scriptures that declare man's true nature as being utterly lost and incapable, how is it possible for anyone to choose or desire God?" The answer is, "He cannot.

Therefore God must predestine." (From http://www. calvinistcorner.com/tulip.htm, Accessed Aug. 9, 2016)

When you carefully read the identified verses, you will not find any specific words or statements that tell us people are incapable of choosing God or righteousness. Yes, these verses identify the characteristics of people without Christ in their hearts, but none of them identify any incapability of choosing God. Desiring to satisfy fleshly lusts and sin does not automatically mean that the capability to choose God is not there. Carefully note that the first sentence of the quote identifies that this Calvinist doctrine is "derived from" these verses. And then carefully note that the statement after the references describes man's true nature as being utter lost "and incapable," this is where the satanic deception comes in. The "and incapable" is an opinion introduced to the discussion when none of the Scripture references identify or describe that "incapability." Then the equally deceptive statement follows, questioning what God already has stated in His word, "how is it possible for anyone to choose or desire God." (See previous reference to Luke 12:;57, and reference to John 1:12 below.)

Before we go any further, let's review our understanding of the word "control." Control is simply "to cause someone or something to behave a certain way or believe a certain thing." The phrase in that definition 'to cause" means "a person or thing that gives rise to (to make something happen or begin, especially something unpleasant or unexpected) an action, phenomenon, or condition" Typically, some sort of force or coercion is involved in control. Now let's take a look at what the Scripture has to say about an aspect of control.

Acts 10:38 (NASB) "*38 You know of Jesus of Nazareth, how God anointed Him with the Holy Spirit and with power, and how He went about doing good and healing all who were <u>oppressed by the devil</u>, for God was with Him.*"

Let's take a close look at that underlined phrase: "oppressed by the devil." The word "oppress" in Greek means, "to exercise power over another," and in this context, it is focused on people, the ones being healed or delivered. An investigation of this word in Greek identifies synonyms such as: "to annoy, trouble, bother," "to treat in an evil way," "to afflict," or "to cause hardship." But, take careful note that exercising power over people is from the devil, not God. This is confirmed by a conversation between Jesus and His disciples in Matthew 20:25-28 and Luke 22:25-27. Here Jesus starts with identifying that the kings of the Gentiles lord it over their people, but it is not that way with the disciples. He then goes on to describe that the greatest in the kingdom of God is the servant of all, and Jesus is among them as a servant.

Deception In Gospel Presentation

I think we can all agree that there is no one greater than God in the kingdom of God. That would make God the greatest servant of all according to the contrast Jesus is presenting in this conversation. Then in John 14:7, 9, Jesus states that if you know or have seen Him (Jesus), you have known or seen the Father. Think of our modern saying, "Like father, like son," in a good sense. Jesus came as a servant, showing that God, the Father is a servant and that is in contrast to the kings of the Gentiles who lord it over their people. To "lord it over" simply means "to domineer, to direct and control someone."

Isaiah 54:15 (NASB) *15 "If anyone fiercely assails you it will not be from Me. Whoever assails you will fall because of you."*

Here, God is not in control of the assailant, nor the Israelites defeating the assailant. So then, God does not use force to control people, Satan is the one that exercises power over people (typically through fear), oppressing them, lording it over people, etc., the opposite of how God behaves. This is not a difficult concept to understand. Realize that when you were born, you grew up under Satan's world system until you found salvation in Jesus, and are now in the process of learning how to function and operate in God's kingdom. That is a huge transformation that needs to take place.

And if you study the three passages about the "Gaderene Demoniac," Mat. 8:28-9:1; Mk. 5:1-

21; Lk 8:28-40, Mark 5:6 states that this man saw Jesus far off and ran to him. There is nothing stated in Scripture that the Holy Spirit had already saved this person and was leading or "controlling" the man to go to Jesus. Even after the man arrived at Jesus' feet, he was still demon possessed, the demons talking through the man negotiating with Jesus to be cast into a herd of swine. Note also, that after the man was delivered, that he was clothed and in his right mind. The use of proper inference here indicates that prior to the man's deliverance he was not in his right mind. Therefore this man, demon possessed and not in his right mind, was capable of choosing Jesus. This is contrary to the Calvinist position. Is your faith based in the truth of what is actually written in God's word, or in satanic opinion that is added to his word?

John 1:12 tells us that God gave people the right to become children of God. The word "right," in Greek, means: "authority, power, the right to govern and control." When you put the definition into the sentence, it tells us that God gave people "the authority, the power, the right to govern and control" becoming a child of God. God gave people the ability to decide their eternal destiny in spite of their depravity prior to the salvation event. As stated above in Acts 10:38, oppression is from the devil, the devil exercises power over another. God never exercises power over those created in His image and likeness*. The Holy Spirit persuades us to change our mind (repent) and believe in our heart on Jesus, and after the Holy Spirit enters our spirit, our being, the Holy Spirit continues to persuade us to do those things that are pleasing to God, and the things that Jesus commanded. There is no force or coercion or direct manipulation from God to get us to follow Him either before or after the salvation event. Every situation we encounter requires us to choose either righteousness or sin. (*Here's a simplistic way of understanding this – if God created Adam as a controlled being, and God created Adam in His image and likeness, then God has to be a controlled being himself. The question then becomes, who or what controls God? Obviously, God is not controlled by anyone or anything, therefore the premise that "God created Adam as a controlled being" is wrong according to the Rule of Logic.)

In these examples of Calvinist philosophy, there is a commonality. That is the use of compound statements, sentences that contain two phrases, or two actual sentences. The first phrase does contain some truth that can be verified by reading the Scriptures. However, the second phrase or sentence is false, and amounts to an opinion that has no support in Scripture; it's not even proper use of inference. Just like in Genesis 3, Satan introduced "you can be your own god" into the conversation, these deceptive modern statements are evidence that Satan is still using this same technique. Just because the first part is true, that does not mean, nor require that the second part is also true.

There is something I call "mental filters" which tend to inhibit the amount of data or information we absorb in any given situation. There are many types of these filters, and they usually are indicative of what our preconceptions are about anything. One of these mental filters I call, "factor of one." I've found this mental filter everywhere I've traveled in the world (at least 14 different countries). We want to reduce every situation down to a "factor of one." What is that one thing in the situation that I can put the blame on for the entire situation? This particular satanic deception requires us to handle two factors, and it cannot be broken down to just one. Our carelessness is what Satan is taking advantage of here. We see the first part of the deception, which usually does contain some truth, and use that as the "factor of one" to define the whole situation or concept or sentence. If that first statement is true, then everything else following must also be true. NOT! That is where Satan deceives us, because of our own carelessness and mental filters. Most of the time, we must balance two factors in a situation, and sometimes three or more.

To be able to see the deception in these examples, we must step "out of our box of mental filters" and understand that the second statement is not necessarily true because the first one seems to be true. Each statement or phrase must be examined on it's own merits (good or bad, true or false).

Truth can only be determined by God's word. We as Christians must find the courage to stand for truth no matter who it is that says or writes something about Christianity, the bible, God, or whatever religious label it falls under. If it doesn't match, at least in principle and concept that which is actually written in the bible, then just simply don't believe it. You might need to do some research into the definitions of words to understand what was said or written, and also to understand what is written in God's word, but take the time to do the research, or at least ask questions of someone you know that has some understanding or access to Greek or Hebrew lexicons. If research still doesn't make things line up together, then God's word is truth, and whatever was said or written is wrong. Don't worry about "offending" someone because they don't line up with God's truth and you are not going to believe it. Telling anyone who doesn't believe on Jesus that they are a sinner is already "offensive." And just because someone went to seminary doesn't make what they say as correct and truthful as God's word.

The thief (Satan, John 10:10) comes only to kill, steal, and destroy. Satan wants to deceive you, to destroy your relation to God and other Christians, and do it in such a way that you don't even suspect the deception is happening. In Acts 17:11, the Bereans examined the Scriptures daily to see if what Paul said is true. Christians must do the same thing – examine the Scriptures daily to see if what is said or written is true. Just because someone can tell a captivating story for a sermon illustration does not make what they say true. Quality in word smithing is not the proper basis for determining truth. Just because there is a phrase that matches up with the bible truth does not mean that everything stated or written regarding that truth is also true. The reality is that Satan can and does use pieces of truth to deceive by wrapping that truth in a context which twists it into something false.

We need to see that God can and does control some things, like demons, and what I call "forces of nature," things not created in God's image and likeness. Jesus controlled demons by speaking to them with His voice. "Forces of nature" can include animals, weather, earthquakes, asteroids, planets, etc. For instance, read the book of Jonah, just a few chapters. In Jonah, God controlled the wind, the storm, the fish, the plant, the worm, and the wind again. God never controlled Jonah. In Genesis, God gave "rule over" to Adam and Eve of:

Genesis 1:26 (NASB) "*26 Then God said, "Let Us make man in Our image, according to Our likeness; and let them rule over the fish of the sea and over the birds of the sky and over the cattle and over all the earth, and over every creeping thing that creeps on the earth."* "

Creeps, creeping thing: (CWSB Dictionary) *"H7431.* רֶמֶשׂ *remeś: A masculine collective noun meaning creeping things, moving things. It describes a large category of living beings that God created. It does not include large animals or birds. It includes many small animals, reptiles, beings that crawl, creep, move randomly, etc., along the earth."*

Please note that "rule over" did not include each other or other people. That is something that gets "read into" the Scripture. In classical logic that is typically called "arguing from absence," making an argument based on no factual evidence, the evidence is "absent." There is something that I have labeled "God's curse on modifying His word." This comes from Deuteronomy 4:2, 18:18-22; Proverbs 30:6; Jeremiah 26:2; and Revelation 22:18-19. These passages tell us that we are to pay attention to all God's word, we are not to omit or leave out any of His word, and we are not to add to God's word. So, if God did not give Adam and Eve "rule over" to each other or other people, God does not want us to "add that into," or "read into" Scripture something He did not state. Think about the aspect of the fruit of the Spirit in Galatians 5 labeled "self-control."

But, what about kings and rulers of government?

Romans 13:3-4 (NASB) *"³ For rulers are not a*

cause of fear for good behavior, but for evil. Do you want to have no fear of authority? Do what is good and you will have praise from the same; [4] for it is a minister of God to you for good. But if you do what is evil, be afraid; for it does not bear the sword for nothing; for it is a minister of God, an avenger who brings wrath on the one who practices evil."

1 Timothy 2:1-2 (NASB) *"[1] First of all, then, I urge that entreaties and prayers, petitions and thanksgivings, be made on behalf of all men, [2] for kings and all who are in authority, so that we may lead a tranquil and quiet life in all godliness and dignity."*

God has placed kings (etc.) in authority as ministers against evil. If you look at the political scene anywhere in the world today and going back as far as the time of Noah after the flood, you will find people in a position of authority that supports evil instead of being against it. Adam and Eve gave the "rule over" to Satan through the temptation of Eve in Genesis chapter 3. This was after the "rule over" was given to Adam and Eve. So we do not find that kings and worldly governments are behaving in a godly manner, but a satanic manner. This is just as Jesus described in Matthew 20 and Luke 22 as discussed above.

Control over people, exercising power over people, lording it over people, causing or using force to make people do things, are all ways of describing Satan's way of doing things in his world system. God's kingdom works differently. God's way is to be the servant of all. There is a way to "rule over" things or people without using forceful control. God does it with persuasion, the vocal and written kind. We'll get to that momentarily.

Some religious philosophies teach that God is sovereign, and that sovereignty requires God to exercise power to control people in various ways. Based on what has been discussed, that kind of sovereignty is satanic, not godly. Some religious philosophies think that we have "free will" to choose God or reject him, but if we choose God, and then surrender an area of our life to God that He then "controls" us in that area. Some would go so far as to say that we still have free will and can take back "control" any time we choose. Unfortunately, God does not change, and the "after-surrender-control" is also a satanic philosophy. There is no "give-and-take" of control back-and-forth between the believer and God. God does not behave in any kind of similar manner as Satan does. For the Christian there then comes the question of what is going on, or how does God's plan for our lives actually come about? The answer is not complicated, there are some details but not too many.

Let's look at the meaning of the word "faith." Most Christians will quote Hebrews 11:1, the substance of things hoped for, the evidence of things not seen. That really does not answer the question, I'm asking for something more basic. In Greek, the word "faith" means, "to have a firm persuasion." That meaning comes from the root of the word "faith," which is the word "persuade." Persuade means, "To persuade, particularly to move or affect by kind words or motives." Note an integral part of persuade requires words, whether spoken or written. Persuasion is the presentation of information (words) that convince (persuade) someone to behave a certain way or believe a certain thing. The presentation of words is not the same as any use of force to cause something. The "cause" involved here is simply presenting the evidence so that someone can decide if it is good or bad information and if it should be believed or not. The presentation of information is not the same as the use of force or exercising power over a person.

Romans 2:8 (NASB) *"8 but to those who are selfishly ambitious and <u>do not obey</u> the truth, but <u>obey</u> unrighteousness, wrath and indignation."*

In Greek, the words translated as "obey" are actually two forms of the word persuade. Using the word persuade in this verse lets it read "but to those who are selfishly ambitious and <u>refuse to be persuaded</u> to the truth, but <u>are persuaded</u> to unrighteousness, wrath and indignation." We can be persuaded to righteousness, or we can be persuaded to unrighteousness. This gives us a huge clue to how things really happen. Both the Holy Spirit and Satan (his demon forces) start with persuasion to convince us of either good or evil thoughts or actions. The big difference between the two results is that with Satan, once the conviction or persuasion is firm in his favor, Satan uses force to maintain the persuasion. This typically includes the use of fear to maintain control. The Holy Spirit continues to use persuasion in love to lead the believer to choose the way of righteousness in every situation. God does not change (Malachi 3:6; Hebrews 13:8; James 1:17), He starts with persuasion and continues with it.

When Christians believe they have free will to choose salvation or not, and then after choosing salvation they surrender an area of their life to God, and God then "controls" that area of their life, they don't realize that the ways of Satan's world system are different than the ways of the kingdom of God. God does not need to forcefully "control" people, believers, to accomplish His plans. We need to examine the difference between God's commands and God's will before we proceed much further. God's presentation of information to persuade us to continue choosing righteousness is a "cause" as in the definition of "control," but it is without the use of fear, force or coercion or direct manipulation. We always have the choice as to follow through with God's desires (will) or not.

Deception In Gospel Presentation

God's commands obviously need to be obeyed. I think it is legitimate to think of this as the General giving orders to His troops. The word in Greek for "will" means, "wish, desire, intent, with no concept of demand." God's commands and God's will are entirely opposite things. Commands do not *require* any love in order to obey. People might obey a command for reasons of self-preservation, they just don't want to get smacked for not obeying. In order to follow through on God's will (or not) requires a love response (or not). We follow through on God's will because we love Him and desire to do things that please Him. This desire to please God is similar to that of a young child that wants to do things that make Mommy and Daddy happy.

Let me give you a hypothetical example to help clarify this. At church on Sunday, we have "children's church" that requires a parent to register the child when they arrive. You are standing in the foyer and see a mother come in with five children. God's command for you in this situation would come across as "Go help that mother get her children registered for children's church." God's will would come across as "It would be pleasing to me if someone would help that mother get her children registered for children's church." The first, the command, would not require any love in order to obey (yes, love would be nice on someone's part, but is not a re-quirement). The second, God's will with no concept of demand, would be followed through with, or not, based on your love response to God. Notice that the end goal is very clear and distinct in both situations, it is the attitude of presentation that makes the difference. One way is an order, the other way is a way of persuasion with no concept of demand. I'm sure that by now you should see the difference. Another thing that we need to examine is love.

In all the descriptions of love in the Scripture, there are no words used that require or imply any form of forceful control. In fact quite the opposite. One of the characteristics of love that we seldom think about is that love is "one way."

1 Corinthians 13:4-8a (NASB) *"4 Love is patient, love is kind and is not jealous; love does not brag and is not arrogant, 5 does not act unbecomingly; it does not seek its own, is not provoked, does not take into account a wrong suffered, 6 does not rejoice in unrighteousness, but rejoices with the truth; 7 bears all things, believes all things, hopes all things, endures all things.*

8 Love never fails..."

The phrase "does not seek its own" could just as easily be translated as "does not seek itself." Real love does not do things or say things in order to derive love from whatever thing or person the love is focused on.

Romans 5:8 (NASB) *"8 But God demonstrates His own love toward us, in that while we were yet sinners, Christ died for us."*

2 Peter 3:9 (NASB) *"⁹ The Lord is not slow about His promise, as some count slowness, but is patient toward you, not <u>wishing</u> for any to perish but for all to come to repentance."*

The word translated "wishing" is the word for "will" that has no concept of demand. The two verses together (plus others) tell us that God sent His Son to die for us with no requirement or demand or expectation that anyone would love him in return in any form or manner. God provided the means of salvation without requiring anyone to love Him in return, or to love Him first before He took action. Love does not seek itself. The point is that there is no requirement for the love response, His love just gives. This in no way negates God knowing beforehand that there would be those who do love Him in return. There is a difference between "knowing" and "forcing," or "decreeing." That love is initiated from themselves, and in no way is forced or coerced.

Will: (CWSB Dictionary) *"2307. θέλημα thélēma; gen. thelématos, neut. noun from thélō (G2309), to will. The suffix -ma indicates that it is the result of the will. Will, <u>not to be conceived as a demand</u>, but as an expression or inclination of pleasure towards that which is liked, that which pleases and creates joy. When it denotes God's will, it signifies His gracious disposition toward something. Used to designate what God Himself does of His* *own good pleasure."*

Note the underlined phrase that "will" is "not to be conceived as a demand." God's will is simply what is pleasing to him. Persuasion is used to bring us to belief on Jesus for salvation and God continues with persuasion after the salvation event. The concept of persuasion "dove-tails" perfectly with the meaning of "will."

Love does not seek itself has some amazing implications for believers. A significant number of passages that mention enduring faith or staying or enduring with faith to the end, only mention the "reward" or "blessing" of eternal life. Paul, in his analogy of living the Christian life is like running a race, tells us that we should run to win the prize. The prize in an imperishable wreath, eternal life (1 Corinthians 9:24-27). A believer's true love response to God's will does not expect any reward or blessing for making that love response. In other words, we don't respond to God's will in order to chalk up "brownie points" with God. Just as God loved us and sent His Son to die for us, when we make a love response to God we should not expect an immediate return on the investment. Yes, we can experience blessings in this life, but to do things "Christian" to get immediate rewards means you have missed the point. Several times Jesus condemned the Jewish leaders for their action that gave them the immediate reward from people, but not from God. James hits the "bull's eye" when he describes in his letter in chapter 2 that our faith is demonstrated, or shown, by our "works," the things we do and our behavior and attitudes. Those "works" are "one way" activities; we are to love others through our actions and words no matter what the response might be.

All the concepts we have examined, command versus will, love is "one way," forceful control is satanic, faith is based on persuasion, etc., are all characteristics of the situation we need to understand in order to find meaning in the fact that God does not use force to control people. God is love, and love does not forcefully control the object of that love. When God persuaded us to choose the way of righteousness in a situation, He brings us to the point of decision and leaves it up to us for that final decision based on our love response to Him. We are the ones responsible for actually committing to the decision either way we choose. If we choose unrighteousness, then we are totally responsible. If we choose righteousness, then we are totally responsible for the decision. God never forcefully "controls" our decisions.

Is your faith in God based on opinion that is added to God's word, or on what is actually written in God's word? In order to understand God's word, we need to pay attention to all that He has provided (said, written, done, made, etc.).We don't have the permission or instruction from God to pick and choose what "pieces" of the bible we use and believe, and ignore the rest. Part of this satanic deception is his "picking and choosing" pieces of God's truth and then mixing his evil opinion with it. If God requires us to pay attention to all His word, then we had better do it. (See Deut. 4:2, 18:18-22; Prov. 30:6; Jer. 26:2; Rev. 22:18-19.) We also need to pay attention to everything that surrounds any pieces of God's truth spoken or written by others to make sure they also match up with God's word. Taking a piece of truth and putting it in a context that is different from the context God used it in, turns that piece of truth into something false. I'm becoming more and more convinced that when people use the phrase "God is in control," it is typically derogatory against God, and is giving credit to the deception from the evil one. The evil one has deceived us into believing it is true, that something never mentioned in Scripture (God controls people created in His image and likeness), something that "sounds godly," is actually giving glory to the wrong god.

The God I worship is so great and sovereign that He can be the greatest servant of all and not have use force or coercion or direct manipulation to control people, and He is the One who will be the winner!

Additional information regarding "God and Control" can be found in my book "*Six Biblical Issues Against "God Is In Control"* ."

Deception In Gospel Presentation